Courage Journal
Sana Turnock

Copyright © Sana Turnock, 2020
Published: 2020 by
The Book Reality Experience
ISBN: 978-0-6489496-0-2
Paperback Edition

All rights reserved.

The right of Sana Turnock to be identified as the author of this Work has been asserted by her in accordance with sections 77 and 78 of the Copyright, Designs and Patents Act 1988.

Whilst every accuracy has been made to fulfil requirements with regard to reproducing data, records and copyright material within this journal, the author and publisher will be glad to rectify any omissions or attributions at the earliest opportunity. Please contact the publisher in the first instance.

The information contained in this journal is of a general nature and should not be regarded as legal advice or relied on for assistance in any particular circumstance or emergency situation. It is not intended as and should not be relied upon for medical advice. The publisher and author are not responsible for any specific health needs that may require medical supervision. If you have any underlying medical or mental health problems, or have any doubts about the advice contained in this book, you should contact a qualified medical, mental health or other appropriate professional.

The Publisher and author jointly or singularly, accept no responsibility or liability for any damage, loss or expense incurred as a result of the reliance on information contained in this guide.

Any third party views or recommendations included in this guide do not reflect the views of the Publisher, or indicate its commitment to a particular course of action.

No part of this publication may be reproduced, stored in a retrieval system, copied in any form or by any means, electronic, mechanical, photocopying, recording or otherwise transmitted without written permission from the publisher.

Cover Design: Web and Print Hub www.webandprinthub.com.au

This journal is dedicated to you, dear journal writer.
Find courage to create the life you want.

Introduction

Welcome to the Courage Journal, a place where you are free to express your deeper yearnings. Whether it is about how you want to live your life, be an amazing business person, be more adventurous or all three – this is your place to do it.

It is a activity-based journal with exercises for you to focus on to help you explore, strengthen and flex your courage muscle.

The aim is to keep writing and stay focussed for at least 12 months on the theme of courage so that you really strengthen your courage muscle. Challenge yourself in positive ways.

What are things you have always wanted to do but never thought you could possibly do? This is the space to explore all of those, to act with positive intentions and undertake practical everyday actions.

You are provided with 14 statements and tasks. Each one takes approximately one month to complete. This could mean writing about things, reflecting, making decisions and acting on what you have written.

There is no order as to where to begin. Simply select a statement and task that captures your attention.

The Courage Journal is a companion to the Courage Unravelled podcast series which can be found at www.courageunravelled.com. I encourage you to listen to the episodes, along with writing in the journal and undertaking the tasks set within.

Wishing you courage in your time of positive transformation.

Love
Sana Turnock

1. It takes courage to step out of your own way and surrender your circumstances to the Universe.

Sometimes you have to stop being the driver of your planned direction because you may be heading in the wrong direction without realising it. This statement is about having the courage to step out of your own way and surrendering your circumstances – especially when everything you have tried is not working.

If you are doing everything you possibly can to achieve something and are still continually hitting roadblocks, take a step back. Over the next 30 days, reassess and evaluate your circumstances. Are you being too controlling? Is it timing? Have you got the right support? Do you need to change strategies?

What would happen if you just 'let go' and see what happens? It takes courage to actually surrender something, especially when you really want it to 'work'. Invite Divine intervention into your life, ask for guidance on where you need to go next and to allow the right people to assist you.

To do this requires clarity on the end goal and seeing it already happen. Put in a timeframe if you wish but don't control the 'how' of the process. Allow this to happen organically.

An example:

There was a period of time where I was wanting to change my work circumstances. I was running a small business and needed part time work to supplement my income as business was really slow. I also wanted to change my current part time job but didn't leave it due to financial circumstances. My thought was I would get another part time job before leaving my current position. I applied for more than 60 jobs over 2 years and got close a few times, but that was about it. Finally, it reached a point where my business folded, I got really sick AND lost my part time job.

What had I kept on doing that wasn't working? I kept on trying to be the captain of my ship and couldn't see another way. I had also been in a niche business for over 20 years. I had a number of skills which I believed were transferrable into other positions. What did I do? I surrendered. I took myself away for a weekend and did mantras, set intentions to clear blockages and be open to invite a new work opportunity that used all my skill sets plus allowed me to develop further professionally. I also did yoga and prayer work. Before the weekend was out, I received a phone call for a job interview in a setting I had not worked in before but had the skills for.

In the end I didn't get that position, but a new part time role was created for me as the interview panel were impressed with my skills and capabilities. This eventually lead, to more work. To this day I am amazed at how I am able to use my skill sets in ways I could never have imagined previously.

It takes courage to surrender your circumstances and simply get out of your own way.

I invite you to try it. Use the next 30 days to work with Universal energy.

Use statements such as 'I am', 'I welcome', 'I invite' – not 'I am going to', 'I wish' or 'I will'.

It takes courage to be creative

– Henri Matisse

It takes courage to be creative

– Henri Matisse

It takes courage to be creative

– Henri Matisse

It takes courage to be creative

– Henri Matisse

It takes courage to be creative

– Henri Matisse

It takes courage to be creative

– Henri Matisse

It takes courage to be creative

– Henri Matisse

Find the courage to confront the dark parts of yourself with kindness and compassion

– Sana Turnock

2. Being a victim is not courageous. It is a contracting energy. Contracting energy blocks flow and abundance and shrinks your ability to live a full life.

Are you ready to make changes to allow flow and abundance in your life? It takes courage to change the old unconscious programs that have been running constantly in your hard drive (you!) for so long.

Creating change is courageous as it can be messy at first before it gets better. For the next 30 days evaluate what you would like to change about yourself or your circumstances. Find the right support service/s to help you do this.

As this is about undoing old programs find someone you resonate with to help you. Working with someone will take more than a month to clear the hard drive of your mind so don't assume it will happen quickly.

What kind of therapies can assist with changing old programs? Some suggestions are hypnotherapy, Reiki, energy work, kinesiology, psychologists/counsellors, body talk and working with horses in a therapeutic way. There are also positive psychology methods such as daily gratitude journaling and specific daily meditation practices.

Find the courage to confront the dark parts of yourself with kindness and compassion

– Sana Turnock

Find the courage to confront the dark parts of yourself with kindness and compassion

– Sana Turnock

Find the courage to confront the dark parts of yourself with kindness and compassion

– Sana Turnock

Find the courage to confront the dark parts of yourself with kindness and compassion

– Sana Turnock

Find the courage to confront the dark parts of yourself with kindness and compassion

– Sana Turnock

Find the courage to confront the dark parts of yourself with kindness and compassion

– Sana Turnock

Find the courage to confront the dark parts of yourself with kindness and compassion

– Sana Turnock

Find the courage to confront the dark parts of yourself with kindness and compassion

– Sana Turnock

It takes courage to surrender your circumstances to the Universe. It takes courage to get out of your own way

– Sana Turnock

3. Being courageous is an expansive energy and opens the heart and mind to live deeply, fully and in your own truth.

Every day for the next 30 days affirm to yourself, 'Today I choose to live courageously' or 'Today I welcome the opportunity to live fully and courageously'. Say your selected affirmation to yourself 'as much as you can twice daily'. Say the affirmation out loud in front of the mirror and write it down. If you feel any emotion go with it and keep saying the affirmation. After 30 days reflect on any changes you have observed within yourself.

It takes courage to surrender your circumstances to the Universe. It takes courage to get out of your own way

– Sana Turnock

It takes courage to surrender your circumstances to the Universe. It takes courage to get out of your own way

– Sana Turnock

It takes courage to surrender your circumstances to the Universe. It takes courage to get out of your own way

– Sana Turnock

It takes courage to surrender your circumstances to the Universe. It takes courage to get out of your own way

– Sana Turnock

It takes courage to surrender your circumstances to the Universe. It takes courage to get out of your own way

– Sana Turnock

It takes courage to surrender your circumstances to the Universe. It takes courage to get out of your own way

– Sana Turnock

It takes courage to surrender your circumstances to the Universe. It takes courage to get out of your own way

– Sana Turnock

It takes courage to surrender your circumstances to the Universe. It takes courage to get out of your own way

– Sana Turnock

4. It takes courage to change and sometimes courage is all you have.

You are ready (or not!) to take a leap into the unknown about a situation, initiative, venture or circumstance. Sometimes your inner drive is the only thing you have and it doesn't seem rational to you or others, but you are compelled forward nevertheless.

To help prepare yourself for your project or situation, over the next 30 days, do your research to the best of your ability. This might mean finding the right support people, working through financials, writing down the benefits and disadvantages and then weighing up the outcome. Speak to appropriate professionals if necessary. Consider factors like timing, family, health and relationships before making a final decision. Is it still worth doing?

It takes courage to create

– Sana Turnock

It takes courage to create

– Sana Turnock

It takes courage to create

– Sana Turnock

It takes courage to create

– Sana Turnock

It takes courage to create

– Sana Turnock

It takes courage to create

– Sana Turnock

It takes courage to create

– Sana Turnock

It takes courage to create

– Sana Turnock

*It takes courage
to change and
sometimes courage is
all you have*

– Sana Turnock

5. It takes courage to simply BE.

Living in Western society is becoming increasingly one of DOING rather than BEING. It takes courage to put the brakes on and just sit in stillness and with patience without being attached to a device. For the next 30 days use silence and your breath as a way to slow yourself down, show loving kindness and patience to yourself. Can you do this without using a device?

At the end of each session (5 min – 30 min) write down your observations. At the end of the 30 days assess how this activity has assisted interactions you have with others and what inner and outer changes have taken place for you.

> It takes courage to change and sometimes
> courage is all you have
>
> – Sana Turnock

It takes courage to change and sometimes courage is all you have

– Sana Turnock

It takes courage to change and sometimes courage is all you have

– Sana Turnock

It takes courage to change and sometimes courage is all you have

– Sana Turnock

It takes courage to change and sometimes courage is all you have

– Sana Turnock

It takes courage to change and sometimes courage is all you have

– Sana Turnock

It takes courage to change and sometimes courage is all you have

– Sana Turnock

It takes courage to change and sometimes courage is all you have

– Sana Turnock

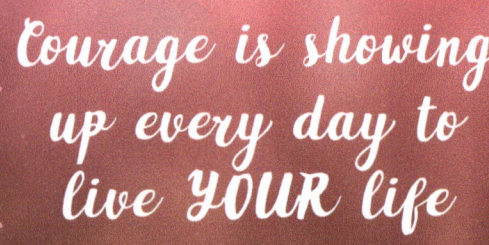

Courage is showing up every day to live YOUR life

– Sana Turnock

6. It takes courage to set boundaries.

Look at all aspects of life – relationships, work, running a business or health. What area/s do you know you could improve your boundaries? Is it around people taking advantage of your time or generosity? Do you feel undervalued or not heard? Is it a friend, family or loved one who continually puts you down? Reflect on your situation. What can you do or say to make a change to the situation? This is about stepping up into your courage. It's your time.

Over the next 30 days when you notice you are being taken advantage of and feel uncomfortable, stand tall in your integrity and speak up. Speak up in a way that will allow you to use your voice in a manner that will not evoke harm for either of you.

Write about the experience and how you felt after exercising your boundary/ies.

Courage is showing up every day to live YOUR life

– Sana Turnock

Courage is showing up every day to live YOUR life

– Sana Turnock

Courage is showing up every day to live YOUR life

– Sana Turnock

Courage is showing up every day to live YOUR life

– Sana Turnock

Courage is showing up every day to live YOUR life

– Sana Turnock

Courage is showing up every day to live YOUR life

– Sana Turnock

Courage is showing up every day to live YOUR life

– Sana Turnock

Courage is showing up every day to live YOUR life

– Sana Turnock

7. **Cultivating your courage muscle takes practise. What are you going to do today to strengthen yours?**

Every day think of something you can do that means cultivating or flexing your courage muscle. It doesn't have to be monumental but it does mean feeling a level of discomfort or challenge in undertaking the activity. After all, courage is about moving through fear and leaning into discomfort in order to grow and develop. Write down your challenge and outcome every day for the next 30 days without judgement of the outcome.

*Courage is knowing when to speak out
and when to stay silent*

– Sana Turnock

Courage is knowing when to speak out and when to stay silent

– Sana Turnock

Courage is knowing when to speak out and when to stay silent

– Sana Turnock

*Courage is knowing when to speak out
and when to stay silent*

– Sana Turnock

Courage is knowing when to speak out and when to stay silent

– Sana Turnock

*Courage is knowing when to speak out
and when to stay silent*

– Sana Turnock

*Courage is knowing when to speak out
and when to stay silent*

– Sana Turnock

*Courage is knowing when to speak out
and when to stay silent*

– Sana Turnock

Courage is reaching out to another without knowing the outcome

– Sana Turnock

8. Step into fear and out of your comfort zone on a regular basis.

Think about what makes you fearful. Write a list and then review it. Are there situations which could put you in genuine danger or are they beliefs or non-threatening situations which bring up fear? It could be a combination.

Choose one or two from your list which you feel you would be willing to commit to move through your fear or discomfort over the next 30-day period. What can you do within the next 30 days to help you move through the fear or discomfort and help you flex and strengthen your courage muscle?

Some suggestions are receiving hypnotherapy, Reiki, energy work, kinesiology, tapping, psychology or counselling sessions. Working with horses in a therapeutic way can also be transforming. Find a meditation practice you can do daily which suits your time frame and one that you believe will promote beneficial outcomes.

*Courage is reaching out to another
without knowing the outcome*

– Sana Turnock

Courage is reaching out to another without knowing the outcome

– Sana Turnock

*Courage is reaching out to another
without knowing the outcome*

– Sana Turnock

Courage is reaching out to another without knowing the outcome

– Sana Turnock

Courage is reaching out to another without knowing the outcome

– Sana Turnock

Courage is reaching out to another
without knowing the outcome

– Sana Turnock

*Courage is reaching out to another
without knowing the outcome*

– Sana Turnock

Courage is reaching out to another without knowing the outcome

– Sana Turnock

It takes courage to be visible

– Sana Turnock

9. Courage is a muscle that needs to be flexed often in order to grow stronger.

Create a courage life list. Think about all the things you want to do but that make you feel challenged, uncomfortable or slightly fearful. These are the things you put on your courage life list. One-by-one start undertaking the activities on your list. Observe how it feels when you complete the first activity, the second and so on. See if you can complete two activities within 30 days. The rest can be done over the course of time.

It takes courage to be visible

– Sana Turnock

It takes courage to be visible

– Sana Turnock

It takes courage to be visible

– Sana Turnock

It takes courage to be visible

– Sana Turnock

It takes courage to be visible

– Sana Turnock

It takes courage to be visible

– Sana Turnock

It takes courage to be visible

– Sana Turnock

It takes courage to be visible

– Sana Turnock

Courage is knowing that things can get messy before transformation takes place – dive in anyway

– Sana Turnock

10. Courage is showing up every day to live YOUR life.

This is not just a sentiment. It really means having the courage to live in a way that stimulates and invigorates you even though it may challenge people close to you. Reflect on how you would really like to live your life. What does it look like? Write it down.

How can you start making it happen today? Start off small and move towards the bigger version of your best life incrementally if it seems a little overwhelming to do so in one go. What kind of a start can you make in the next 30 days?

Tick off what you do and put a date next to it. A photo could be good too!

Courage is knowing that things can get messy before transformation takes place - dive in anyway

– Sana Turnock

Courage is knowing that things can get messy before transformation takes place - dive in anyway

– Sana Turnock

Courage is knowing that things can get messy before transformation takes place - dive in anyway

– Sana Turnock

Courage is knowing that things can get messy before transformation takes place - dive in anyway

– Sana Turnock

Courage is knowing that things can get messy before transformation takes place - dive in anyway

– Sana Turnock

Courage is knowing that things can get messy before transformation takes place - dive in anyway

– Sana Turnock

Courage is knowing that things can get messy before transformation takes place - dive in anyway

– Sana Turnock

Courage is knowing that things can get messy before transformation takes place - dive in anyway

– Sana Turnock

Courage helps you grow and connect with yourself and others

— Sana Turnock

11. Courage is knowing when to speak and when to stay silent.

Over the next 30 days observe your responses and reactions to conversations and things you hear. Do you really need to offer your opinion or give unsolicited advice or are you suppressing your voice due to fear of judgement or being harmed? Timing can be powerful.

Courage helps you grow and connect with yourself and others

– Sana Turnock

Courage helps you grow and connect with yourself and others
– Sana Turnock

Courage helps you grow and connect with yourself and others

– Sana Turnock

Courage helps you grow and connect with yourself and others

– Sana Turnock

Courage helps you grow and connect with yourself and others

– Sana Turnock

Courage helps you grow and connect with yourself and others

– Sana Turnock

Courage helps you grow and connect with yourself and others

– Sana Turnock

Courage helps you grow and connect with yourself and others

– Sana Turnock

12. It takes courage to be a spiritual warrior in business and life.

Write down a version of yourself that you would like to become. Are you currently moving towards your future self or is it a long way off? Reflect on what you are doing, can do or need to do to become your future self.

To be a spiritual warrior is to go inward deeply. Get assistance from healers and work with mentors and professionals to propel you forward.

Over the next 30 days make a start to find ways to get to know yourself. By doing this you will have a genuine capacity to truly connect with others and be able to help them. This is not a 30-day exercise, but an inward journey which takes years to master. Taking the first step of knowing the self is a great start. If you have been doing this already, go deeper.

You grow by being courageous

– Sana Turnock

You grow by being courageous

– Sana Turnock

You grow by being courageous

– Sana Turnock

You grow by being courageous

– Sana Turnock

You grow by being courageous

– Sana Turnock

You grow by being courageous

– Sana Turnock

You grow by being courageous

– Sana Turnock

You grow by being courageous

– Sana Turnock

13. It takes courage to be visible.

You want to stand tall in your visibility but are afraid. What's holding you back? Courage encourages you to look into your fear and work through it.

There are many ways to be visible in the world. This includes being in business. It could be through video, blogging, vlogging, writing articles, networking, running groups, writing, being creative and showing off your work, exhibiting, going into competitions, undertaking dance classes, public speaking, being in a play, singing – the list goes on.

Choose one, two or more activities from the above. For the next 30 days do daily visibility activities. Make them enjoyable so that any anxiety or fear that arises is minimised or can be better managed as the month moves along. After 30 days, reflect on your experience. What did you learn?

It takes courage to set boundaries

– Sana Turnock

It takes courage to set boundaries

– Sana Turnock

It takes courage to set boundaries

– Sana Turnock

It takes courage to set boundaries

– Sana Turnock

It takes courage to set boundaries

– Sana Turnock

It takes courage to set boundaries

– Sana Turnock

It takes courage to set boundaries

– Sana Turnock

It takes courage to set boundaries

– Sana Turnock

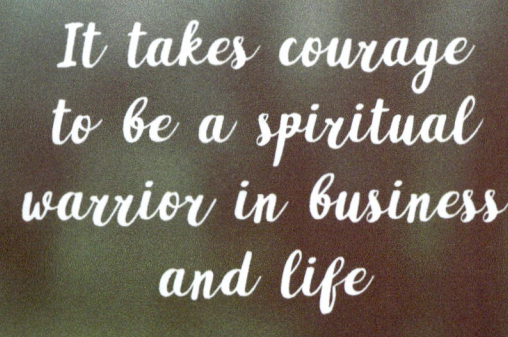

It takes courage to be a spiritual warrior in business and life

– Sana Turnock

14. Courage is knowing that things can get messy before transformation takes place. You dive in anyway.

You want to change something. It can be a situation, a behaviour or pattern. Find a time every day (early morning before anyone else is up is best) and dedicate 15 minutes to writing about what you have selected. Allow whatever it is to come out. It can be anything in written form: journal-style writing, poetry, stream-of-consciousness (pouring out whatever is in your head onto the page), affirmations and/or I am statements. You write without judgement of spelling, grammar or whether or not you think your writing makes sense. At the end of the 15 minutes, write down five things you are grateful for. After the 30 days review your situation, pattern or behaviour. What has changed?

It takes courage to be a spiritual warrior in business and life

– Sana Turnock

It takes courage to be a spiritual warrior in business and life

– Sana Turnock

It takes courage to be a spiritual warrior in business and life

– Sana Turnock

It takes courage to be a spiritual warrior in business and life

– Sana Turnock

It takes courage to be a spiritual warrior in business and life

– Sana Turnock

It takes courage to be a spiritual warrior in business and life

– Sana Turnock

It takes courage to be a spiritual warrior in business and life

– Sana Turnock

It takes courage to be a spiritual warrior in business and life

– Sana Turnock

Living your best life takes takes courage

– Sana Turnock

About the author

Sana grew up in Perth, Western Australia and as a child loved to draw, read and write stories. Sana kept a diary from the age of 12 into her adult life and wrote a secret novella (which no-one ever saw) when she was a teenager.

Over the years Sana has trained in the areas of clinical aromatherapy, holistic health care, aged and palliative care and adult education. She has published a couple of books and her articles have appeared in industry journals. She holds a Master of (Adult) Education, and Diplomas in various natural therapy modalities.

Like a lot of Australians, Sana has lived overseas and travelled to many countries but still finds the South West of Western Australia her favourite place to live.

An avid learner and appreciator of beauty, Sana loves being in nature, walking and hiking. She is also partial to movies, laughing, dancing and singing with her daughter and spending time with her loving family and gorgeous dog.

Sana works on training and flexing her courage muscle so that she can live a meaningful life.

To find out more about Sana and what she offers go to
www.courageunravelled.com

Acknowledgments

Big thanks and gratitude to Julie (Jules) Rick for helping me manifest my creative vision. I love her graphic design skills and working with her. What a professional!

To Ian and Jasmine at Book Reality and Leschenault Press for making the publishing of this journal possible.

Finally, to my loving family for putting up with me spending many hours in the office dreaming up big dreams (that live inside my head). You are what motivates me to do what I do. Big love.

www.ingramcontent.com/pod-product-compliance
Lightning Source LLC
Chambersburg PA
CBHW040742020526
44107CB00084B/2841